THE IRS
Dirty Little Secrets

Copyright © 2023 - Patrick Rood

Published by Rood Financial Services

1st EDITION

ISBN: 979-8-218-12318-5

Printed in the United States of America

ALL RIGHTS RESERVED. This book contains material protected under International and Federal Copyright Laws and Treaties. Any unauthorized reprint or use of this material is prohibited. No part of this book may be reproduced or transmitted in any form or by any means, electronic or mechanical, including photocopying, recording, or by any information storage and retrieval system without express written permission from Laurie Kathryn Grant, the author, and publisher, except for non-commercial uses as permitted by copyright law.

The information in this book is provided for information purposes and is intended to be only general guidelines. This book is not intended to give any legal, medical, and/or financial advice to the reader. While every effort has been made to verify the information provided, neither the author nor the publisher assumes any responsibility for any errors, omissions, or incorrect interpretations of the subject matter contained herein. The reader assumes responsibility for their use of this information. The reader cannot hold the author responsible or liable for any actions they take or the results of those actions.

SIGNING PAGE

TABLE OF CONTENTS

SIGNING PAGE 5
INTRODUCTION 9

CHAPTER I: The Secret Hiding in Plain Sight 15
Secret Hiding 17
Do You Have Control of Your Money? 19
Income Taxes: Do You Decide or Does Government? 20
Do You Have Options? 22
The Tax Code Purpose 24

CHAPTER II: Illuminating or Illuminati? 28
Is There a Conspiracy to Oppress You? 31
You Are in Control of Your Life and Finances 33
Being Manipulated for Spending 35

CHAPTER III: The Proof is in The Pudding 40
Follow the Money 43
The Financially Comfortable 45
The Financially Free 46
What Do the Super Wealthy Know and Practice? 48
Financial Ninjitsu 51

CHAPTER IV: When You Know Better-You Do Better .54
Knowledge is Power Manifesting in Money and Respect 56
Money Follows Attention 58
Respect Follows Integrity 60

CHAPTER V: Structure is Key 63
Choosing Your Business Vehicle and Tax Benefits 65
LLC 67
Partnership 68

    S-Corp 69

    Corporation/C Corp 71

CHAPTER VI: Loophole Benefits 75

    What Tax Loopholes Can You Legally Take Advantage of?. 77

    Augusta Loophole 78

    Self Employed Health Insurance Credit 79

    Bonus Depreciation and Section 179 Deductions 80

CHAPTER VII: Evasion Versus Avoidance 83

    Taxes Are Mandatory When You Don't Spend Correctly 87

CHAPTER VIII: Do Not Perish for Lack of Knowledge . 92

    Find Someone to Advise You 95

    A True Leader Gathers Experts 97

Thank You 100

INTRODUCTION

"Every adventure will contain experiences you would never want."
-Grant Cardone

For many years I have worked with companies across the country, helping them lower their tax liability, handling many complex tax situations, and, most of all, helping them grow their business.

But before we get into this book, I first want to take you to what inspired me to start my business and begin helping people grow their businesses and ultimately accomplish their dreams.

When I was in high school, my father decided to start his own business. He had spent 30 years working in his field, where he became one of the best at plastic extrusion. He had now reached the point where most people also arrived to become entrepreneurs. At this point, you get tired of making everyone else rich while you struggle to survive.

My father had no college education; he was a self-made man. He had a dream for our family, and his education was from the School of Hard Knocks in the profession he was trying to turn into his own manufacturing business. He had worked with large automakers such as Ford, General Motors, Chrysler, and Hyundai, so they were already familiar with some of his work because of the projects he had worked on during his employment with other manufacturers.

These relationships would have allowed him to start his business from nothing and grow it over six years to a multimillion-dollar Enterprise. As most people understand these days, it is vital to be selective about the people you surround yourself with, and the trust you place in these advisors can be Paramount when starting your business.

Some of you know there are three vital components that you need when you're starting your own business the first is a good Banker, the second is a good accountant, and the third is a good lawyer. These are your power players, and they will help you keep your business in compliance and help you with the most complicated matters, especially regarding your finances and the government.

I don't know about the banker my father had; to my knowledge, he didn't have a proper accountant, and my father did not particularly trust lawyers. In these three aspects, he was sorely lacking. If there had been a better method and someone who was an unbiased third party that could have advised my father about dealing with the IRS in dealing with situations that can sometimes arise when you're late filing returns or when you don't pay your taxes, he would still be in business to this day. But unfortunately, he did not have this third-party advisor he desperately needed.

He had to close his firm, sell his equipment to one of his clients, and work for them while he paid the IRS off after they contacted him about issues with underpayment and failure to file returns. My parents did all they knew how to do; they kept good books, learned QuickBooks, and tried to hire people, but in the end, no one could give my parents the advice they needed to keep their business. So, it went under, and we closed our doors. I will never forget, as stressful as it was sometimes, the joy that we had and the adventures that we were able to have because my father owned his own business and all the headaches that came along with it.

My father would have to come to work when any of the employees called out and helped run the show. He jumped right in on the line. Sometimes my sister and I would jump in along with him, but we were still very young, so there was only so much we could do in a factory. There were nights when we had slumber parties in the office, sleeping in sleeping bags underneath desks because my father and mother had to work the third shift because someone had shown up drunk or called in sick.

It was a great experience as a young person. To see the possibility of what you can build with nothing more than your knowledge and your imagination. It was also a testament to what stress can do to you. My father ended up in the hospital having mini-strokes just before the company was going to close. Nearly having a mild heart attack or near heart attack, I don't remember which, but those were scary times. I remember worrying about what would happen to my father and our future.

I didn't even know half of what was going on. My parents did such a good job protecting us. Yes, we knew my father was sick. We knew my father was having health issues. We were unaware that they were related to stress and the closing of the business. My father always paid his employees first and ensured our family never went without, even when he was losing money.

Because of that, I respect my father as a man, an entrepreneur, and a provider. However, growing up with my father wasn't always easy. He has some anger issues, but he never abused me and my sister or my mother. Now, as a father, my anger is one of the things I work on, ensuring my son knows how much I love him, just like my father made sure I knew how much he loved me. I want to do better than my father and make sure that my son sees his father dealing with his anger healthily and learns to be a better man because of me. Now you may be wondering what this has to do with the IRS's dirty little secrets.

Well, the truth is that this all has to do with why I'm writing this book and why I became a tax strategist and fractional CFO. I wanted to give other people the opportunity to succeed in their businesses, which my parents never had. I wanted to give people the advisor that my parents needed but never had the opportunity to come in contact with them.

This is why I started my tax practice, became an international award-winning Author, and became a Grant Cardone licensee & certified 10X coach and speaker.

Well, the truth is that this has to do with why I'm writing this book and why I became a tax strategist and fractional CFO. I wanted to give other people the opportunity to succeed in their businesses, which my parents never had. I wanted to give people the advisor my parents needed but never had the fortuity to have.

It is why I started my tax practice, became an international award-winning Author, and became a Grant Cardone licensee, certified 10X coach and speaker. There are other people out there that can do what I do absolutely, but we are few and far between.

Today anybody can file taxes; millions of people do it on their own through TurboTax or other software every year. Some people can help maintain your books, your QuickBooks or your financials, but very few people know the tax code; and its practical applications and who know how to work with the IRS to avoid situations like what my father and my family went through.

So before getting into this book, I wanted you to get an idea of who I am, why I do what I do, and why it is my greatest passion. Many of you who know me personally have heard me say my mission is to screw the IRS out of his much money legally every year as possible. As Dave Ramsey says, millions of people give an interest-free loan to the government every single year needlessly.

As Grant Cardone says, if you aren't operating in some business, you are just giving away money. As Robert Kiyosaki says, you have to learn the power of cash flow and how it affects your life, business, and taxes, and once you understand that, you can attain true freedom. So I invite you, friends, to come on this journey with me to learn how to take control of your finances and learn the dirty little secrets hidden in plain sight that aren't Secrets at all.

It's just that no one has been communicating things the way that I'm going to tell you in this book, in a way that's easily digestible and personally applicable to your life and shows you how to take advantage of what's available to you so you can set yourself up to win in life and business.

CHAPTER I:
The Secret Hiding in Plain Sight

Secret Hiding

Most people don't realize it, but there's a secret hiding in plain sight. What that secret really is, it's just knowledge. It's not really a secret at all. The secret is that the law gives you every right to control your money and taxes. I frequently tell people that the tax code is setup to support business owners rather than the average worker.

When most people hear the word entrepreneur, they think of people in business for themselves. People that may have a brick-and-mortar store, in network marketing or even those who may have an online-based venture. I would consider anyone who receives a 1099 or money from sources outside their control and the government does not initially tax to be an entrepreneur. Only these individuals control their money, finances, and, eventually, taxes.

You may not believe this but let me assure you this is true. The best explanation can be found in "The Cashflow Quadrant" by Robert Kiyosaki, where he discusses money flow. He is referring to the fact that when you work as an employee, you receive a salary, with your taxes automatically withheld, and then you pay your bills with the money left over. I haven't found a better illustration of the truthful and straightforward way wealth and income flow.

He then explains how businesses operate with cash flow and taxes. The surprising thing about his theories is they are almost the opposite of what people believe. If you can understand this one simple fact, you will begin to gain control of your finances and, ultimately, the trajectory of your life. That may sound like a big claim but let me tell you why when a business earns revenue, it spends "business expenses," and afterwards, you pay tax on what is left over. However, the good news about being in business is that you don't have to have anything left over and especially with the way the tax code is currently, you can buy things that can cause you to lose money on paper which can potentially provide you with extra cash flow that could not be taxed.

Many people understand they have to pay their taxes quarterly when they are an entrepreneur or in business. In some cases, you may need to pay quarterly taxes. Still, it is not always required to pay quarterly taxes. To avoid this, ensure you don't show a profit at the end of the year, or you must pay at least 90% of the prior year's liability if you do have a profit.

This method will remove any need for you to pay quarterly payments ever. A lot of people get worried when it comes to paying taxes. The truth is you need to be aware of the deadlines on the timelines for when you need to pay those taxes. However, wouldn't it be better if you could ensure you didn't have to pay taxes at all? I can hear some people saying, " Oh my gosh, that's illegal tax evasion, and you're right, evasion of taxes is very criminal."

You should never avoid paying your taxes; instead, leverage the tax code to reduce the amount of taxes you owe, from thousands to having to pay zero dollars or even to the point where the IRS owes you money. These methods are in black and white within the 26000 pages of our US tax code. There lie the means for you to take control of your money and your finances to the point where you never have to be afraid of the IRS or what you may be beholding to them forever again.

This secret is hiding in plain sight because the tax code is available for anyone to read or study, but it's not taught in our schools, not at home, and trust me, it's barely taught in college. Now, you may be asking, where do I get this information? How do I ensure:

- I'm not paying more tax than I have to

- I'm not afraid to address issues with the IRS
- I have complete control over my money
- No one, including the IRS, can dictate where my money goes.

Then buckle up, my friends; you are in the right spot; that's what this book is for, and ultimately this book will give you the confidence and the tools to take back your financial control.

Do You Have Control of Your Money?

One of the biggest questions people don't even think to ask is who has control of my money. Most employees go to work to earn their salary or hourly wage, wait for that check at the end of the week and then use that money to support their lifestyle. One of the things that most employees are not considering is that they're not even getting to see their entire salary.

Having employees is one of the most important aspects of a business, and while I'm not against having employees, employers in this country and this economy are doing a dismal job of educating our staff so that they have options for securing their financial futures as well as their present ones.

This lack of knowing their options is why 62% of gen Z and 56% of millennials have had a side hustle since 2020. That is more than half of both gen Z and millennials; they're catching on to this fact, and these are employees, not just people starting new businesses. According to US Census data, the number of new ventures has increased by 42% since 2020. These numbers indicate that many individuals are catching on and figuring out how to manage their money.

The unfortunate part is that most of these people don't realize that they can leverage these two factors being an entrepreneur with a side hustle or side business and being a W-2 employee, to essentially gain financial control over where their money is going. The reason most people don't necessarily know this is that it's not taught in school. Who do you consult with if you want to understand how to develop your financial intelligence and make money work for you instead of working for money? The answer is that those who work in finance should impart that knowledge.

The main reason I am in business personally is to educate people about their finances, their income, and how to leverage that to work for them instead of just scraping by.

Income Taxes: Do You Decide or Does Government?
To better understand whether you or the government are in control, we need to discuss income taxes. What are income taxes? The simple explanation is they are taxes levied on the taxable income you earn as designated by the US tax code. As I mentioned before, as an employee, you do not have control over when to pay these taxes. You don't get to decide when the government gets its money; they will always take their pound of flesh first.

I'm sure that's an expression that some of you have heard. However, the tax code gives you explicit instructions on taking back this control by learning to play the game that the wealthy have been playing for years. Now you ultimately have the decision to make. Do you want to wake up, take control of your financial future, and learn how to play the game, or do you want to not think about it? Do you want it to run on autopilot? Do you want to be a victim of a lack of information?

There are always two options to choose from on any matter in life, to take responsibility or avoid responsibility. Ultimately that is what every choice is. You hear people say all the time, especially in the coaching and Guru space and all that jazz. They shout it from the rooftops. Grant Cardone says quite often you are responsible for everything in your life, everything that has happened to you, and everything that is going to happen to you.

The crux of the problem, or rather the choice in the matter, comes with whether you are going to take responsibility for it which means that you can ultimately change it, or are you going to allow it to change you and avoids taking responsibility for everything and remain a victim to your circumstances. Now that may be a very harsh stance but hear me out; how can you control a natural disaster? Sometimes you can't control the amount of devastation you experience, but you can manage your response to that experience.

You can control your output. When bad things happen, how do you respond:

- With oh woe is me?
- What am I going to do?
- How can I do this?

You know nothing's going to get better if its woe is me. When you respond to that attitude, there is nothing to be done; you're stuck. You are now the victim, and when people play the victim or choose to be the victim in their life, it comes with a certain level of entitlement that they believe now the world owes them something to right this injustice.

Are you going to respond with gratitude? As Gary Vaynerchuk talks about, are you going to respond with, "man, that was awful, but I'm alive, and as long as I have my life, I have an opportunity?" The choice is yours. Will you accept accountability for your actions and reactions, or will you run away and let things happen to you? Where this ties in financially, especially with taxes, is very simple, and it just takes one question - what are my options?

Do You Have Options?

What are your options? What can you do? The government and the IRS are humongous and powerful; how could I ever stand up to them taking my money and not giving me control over it? Fortunately, my friends, the answer is simple, it's in the tax code controlling you.

Now you may say, it's not like I can go to my boss and tell him, hey, stop taking taxes out of my paycheck; in fact, I would suggest this is very much a bad idea, and if you think well, it's simple, I know how to get around this I'll claim exempt on my W-4, this is also a bad idea. The reason that this is a bad idea is that, wow, you want to regain control over your finances and gain control over the flow of your own money by opting to have employee an employer relationship and being a W-2 employee; you have agreed that anything you trade your time for money for creating a taxable event you owe taxes on that money.

Now there may be some people out there that say wow, never be an employee again or may respond strongly to this statement and say I will be screwed to be an employee. I hate getting screwed over. Please don't go there; employees are the most valuable asset in our economy and any business. I am not encouraging you to have a mass exodus or leave your employer, to leave your company and stop being an employee unless that's your dream.

If that is your dream, then, by all means, quit but don't quit until you have figured out a way to earn money outside of that job. In every case, in every situation, the best investment and the best bet you can make is an investment and to bet on you, but being an entrepreneur is truly not for everyone.

It comes with a lot of heartache and stress, which can:
- Send you to the hospital
- Destroy your life
- Destroy your health
- Destroy your mind

So, take this warning well; being a true entrepreneur is not for the faint of heart.

We'll get into that later on. I want to demonstrate that you have choices; the government may be enormous and frightening, but the same rules that give it authority also offer us, the people, more power. We elect people that put these laws in place. Unfortunately, the education surrounding these laws and the communication of their application to the public is lacking in so many aspects, and it's likely why you picked up this book today because you feel stuck you want to know how to play the game the way the wealthy play.

The only difference between you and the people who are super-wealthy in this country are three things:

- Your connections or your network,
- Your mindset, and
- Your knowledge.

Those are the only things currently limiting you from reaching your full potential. So, what are your options? Is it better to understand your options and know how to leverage the same tactics, policies, loopholes, and benefits that the super-wealthy take advantage of; you need to understand the purpose of the tax code and how to leverage it to your full potential.

The Tax Code Purpose

To understand something fully, you need to be able to teach it; this has been ingrained in my head and my life through experience time and time again. So, right now, I'm going to discuss the purpose of the tax code, and as they say in some church circles, I will help you understand the heart of the law versus the letter of the law. The tax code is over 26,000 pages long, which is massive.

We have one of the most complicated taxation systems in the entire world. And don't take my word for it; Time magazine or time.com wrote an article about it in 2016. An article about how we have one of the highest rates and most complex tax codes globally. I wish this weren't the case, but there are always loopholes where there is complexity, so it's not all bad.

The tax code always has loopholes that enable individuals to use the law to their advantage rather than being restricted by it. The tax code's primary goal is to redistribute wealth, which is among the first things you need to grasp about it. To better appreciate the enormity, you need to understand some of the numbers in the US; for example, Americans filed 112,254,000 tax returns in 2019.

To understand why that number is significant, let's compare how many people file tax returns based on the number of the US population. There are 328,329,000 people in the USA as of 2019, and the number of adults aged 18 and above is 255,241,278. That means less than half of the US filed a tax return in 2019. With only half the population filing taxes, you can see that these taxes don't go towards anything.

We could have abolished income tax today, and there would be no recourse on our government spending. There would be no effect at all. Do you understand that the reason that we have income tax paid is just federal income tax? We're not looking at social security, Medicare, state tax, local tax, disability family or unemployment. Honestly, it's all a scam, in my opinion. We are only talking about federal income tax, so your federal income taxes are used to pay out refunds to other taxpayers, which is why it is the primary form of wealth redistribution in this country.

Naturally, since the wealthy understand and can afford the advisors to coach them on how to structure their life, their businesses, and their finances around this code, they're not the ones paying income tax. All of us who are W-2 employees and aren't leveraging the tax code as business owners are the ones that are paying for the redistribution of income tax to other people. The tax code, initially, was a temporary measure to raise money for the American Civil War and was a flat 3% tax on all incomes over $800. It became law in 1861.

This tax was initially put in place to aid the country's and the government's recovery from the horrors of the Civil War. Since then, it has been leveraged for specialised interests and personal gain while being distorted and misused. When it comes to the law's spirit, you must understand that while it is possible for tax laws to harm you, you also have equal rights, equal opportunities, and a responsibility to use the law for your benefit as well as the benefit of those in your community and those around you.

Let's face it there is so much you could do in your community. So much you could do in your family. So much more you could do for your brothers and sisters and those less fortunate if you were the one taking personal responsibility for them instead of allowing that responsibility to be on the government. But the only way that you can do that is if you are financially secure.

To attain Financial Security, you have to Achieve Financial intelligence and financial control and start benefiting from the laws you currently do not use. The one thing I want to drive home to everyone who reads this book is that the law is there to guide you, protect you, and ultimately Above All Else, serve you. Lawmakers enact laws for purposes like this, including the tax code.
If you pay attention to new laws when they come out, specifically around the tax code, you will see where the government wants to incentivize spending. You will see the areas of the economy where they want you to invest. For example, when President Trump wrote the tax cuts and jobs act, he lowered tax brackets for all working individuals; he also increased child tax credits for all parents in the US and added two gigantic things, Section 179 deduction and bonus depreciation.

These changes in and of themselves allowed people businesses primarily to deduct the purchase of a vehicle over 6000 lbs 100% in the first year. The trick is that you can finance the entire purchase price of that vehicle for 5, 7, or 8 years and still write off 100% of the purchase price. That was a massive change, and the Congress at the time, along with President Trump, were showing you where they want you to invest, where they want you to spend your money, and how they're going to incentivize you to do so.

Similarly, President Biden's inflation reduction Act features key provisions to keep funding for solar and alternative energy projects. They also open up the solar market and tax credits to not-for-profits, which is new and involves the government encouraging you to invest and spend your money in the places they want you to. That reasoning leads to the only logical conclusion that they incentivize you to become an entrepreneur and that if you don't have a side hustle or start your own business in some way, shape, or form, you are losing money, losing freedom, and holding yourself back because they keep rewarding people in the business space even though business is dead.

In light of this, you may say, well, why would I not become an entrepreneur? As I said, it's not for everyone, but if you want to obtain some form of financial success or gain control over your money and your life, there aren't many better options.

"The word accounting comes from the word accountability. If you are going to be rich, you need to be accountable foryour money."

- Robert Kiyosaki

CHAPTER II:
Illuminating or Illuminati?

There are some people that believe that the government is out to get them. I am not necessarily one of those people; however, I am also not ignorant of the fact that the government controls information, and as any governing body would, they would alter the flow of information in order to protect the people that they are serving. All of that to say, I am not a tinfoil hat kind of guy about this, and this is not a tinfoil hat kind of book.

The reason that the saying knowledge is power exists is that if you are ignorant of the world around you and you don't know what you stand for or what to stand on, then you can literally fall for anything. There are many, many "Theories" surrounding the super wealthy and how they maintain their wealth and seem to pay little to no tax. Ultimately the decision is yours.

Are you going to illuminate your mind and open your understanding of what's available to you and change your behavior so you can start doing things that the super wealthy do, or are you going to keep blaming it on the Illuminati? If you're going to keep blaming the things that go on, something like the Rothschilds or the Illuminati, and just, so we get this out right now, I'm not saying that they don't control everything, then you aren't taking responsibility for your education.

And that is something that every successful person has done. You are no different; you have to pay your dues, and you have to educate yourself. You need to be the person that breaks the curse of property in your family, breaks the curse of poverty in your generation, don't leave a legacy to your children, your children's children, into the generations that come after you of mediocrity. Now, if you don't have any Grand Ambitions in life, that's fine; there is nothing wrong with that, but ultimately the life you live and the generations that come after you and the lies that they live and the start that they receive is a direct result of the choices that you're making in your life here and now.

Is There a Conspiracy to Oppress You?

Now let's talk about the fact that everything in the media and everything around us constantly say that there is something. Some unnamed boogeyman, something out there, is designed to take advantage of you and oppress you and keep you purposefully under their thumb. You can listen to thousands of podcasts about this very fact. You can listen to Alex Jones rant and rave about god-knows-what. He rants about anything and everything.

You can listen to Jordan Peterson talk about speaking for the marginalized, and I love Jordan Peterson. I think he is a phenomenal human being, but the truth is that the only ones doing any kind of oppression are you and I. We're doing it to each other, and the more that we allow the division to end the noise, influence us, and get us to see each other more or less than the collective human race, the more we are going to continue to have problems.

I promise you that there is no specific force out there in the ubiquitous galaxies, government, or society that is specifically trying to impress you as an individual. This does not mean that you will not feel oppression; this does not mean that you will not feel pushback when you start to succeed and when you start to get out of place; that is only a natural feeling. One of the greatest examples that I have ever known came while I was crab fishing.

If anyone does not know what crab fishing is, you take a wire mesh cage with some bait in it could be a turkey neck, could be a fish head, it could be anything you put the bait in the Trap, and then you throw it into the wide water with a string attached to it, and you wait. minuteAnd sometimes if it's a clear day you can see the Trap, and you can see the crabs trying to crawl into the Trap and naturally try to get out of it. The interesting thing comes when you pull the Trap out of the water.

Can you get the crabs into a bucket? Ultimately you will always have crabs trying to escape, but then also you will have crabs that are underneath them that continually pull them back down so that they cannot Escape. This is the greatest analogy for how human beings interact with one another when it comes to success that I have ever seen in my entire life. You may have some people who, for your success, are the people that you keep around, but I guarantee you that you will also have people that, to your face, say they wish for your success but then also try to pull you back down, and they may not even realize that they're doing it and that's the sad part.

The craziest part of all of this is that worth old, and we're taught that it's the systems around us that are designed to keep us down that they're giving some people an unfair advantage and other people they're keeping at a disadvantage. The flat-out truth is this is not the case; as I said before, the only thing that separates anyone is knowledge and understanding. Once you understand that no matter who you are and where you're from, you have the capacity.

That capability of leveraging everything that the super wealthy have at their disposal, you also have it yours, and maybe even more at your disposal than what other people have once you realize that you stop looking at things from a victimhood mentality and you start taking responsibility for where you're going I promise you, your life will change. Your finances will also change. You're going to have to make hard choices about whom you surround yourself with. The people that are keeping you where you are often are not the people that you will have around you when you become successful.

Sometimes that's the price you have to pay for that success is losing those relationships, and for a lot of people, that's a very hard pill to swallow. I had to do it myself. I have friends that I thought were going to be lifelong friends, brothers, and sisters, not by Blood but by a deeper Bond choice. They were collectively making choices that were going to lead to my imprisonment or my death if I continued to associate with them and make similar kinds of choices and decisions for my life. I had no choice but to leave those relationships and keep those people at arm's length and love them from afar so that I could provide a future four generations of my family that was not going to be littered with pain, Brokenness, failure, poverty I've made a choice that I'm going to leave a legacy of healing success winning and prosperity.

You Are in Control of Your Life and Finances
So far in this book, I talked a lot about personal responsibility taking that responsibility for your choices taking responsibility for your life, and ultimately taking responsibility for where you're going to end up. The truth is you're in control of your finances and your life; every decision that you make impacts both those things sometimes in a minute or microscopic ways, but still, they are affected.

As I said in the previous section, there is no one thing person, organization, entity or government, or system trying to purposefully hold you as an individual back which means the only thing that is holding you back is in your head, and if the secret to all of your future success is locked away in your head then don't you think you should spend more time trying to Free Your Mind and increase your knowledge and education, and I'm not talking collegiately, rather than wasting time in the ways that you're currently wasting it.

Because let's face it, we always time everyone scrolling rules on social media endlessly hour after hour after hour while they're supposed to be working. People watch TV when they're supposed to be doing work or when they're actually doing work at home, and they're still watching TV anyways. We sat our children down in front of the TV; very few of us actually read or listen to books anymore. But those are commentaries for a different time.

One thing that I want to make sure that you understand is that you have control over where your life has gotten you and where your life is going to go. You also have control over the finances you have in the bank, the balance in your bank, and where your life is right now. The hard truth is that your success is a direct result of the decisions that you have made in your life to this point. I cannot tell you how many people I have heard; now, as a church person, I am not trying to bash church people, but I have heard people say this, and this is a lie straight from the pit of Hell.

My bank account is overdrawn, my debit card is lost, and I know this is just the devil trying to keep me down and affect me. If you have said, these statements wake you up Because, let me tell you right now, you are responsible for that lost debit card; you are responsible for not being frugal and accurate with your spending. The devil didn't make you do it; your lack of responsibility and discipline made you do it; that is the cold honest truth.

Now I apologize if that offends you but get over it and start taking responsibility for yourself. You are in control of your life; you are in control of your finances. Ask yourself the question, do I want to be in control of my life and my finances, or do I want someone else to be in control of it for me so then I can complain when I am not at the level that I want to be because then it's not really my fault it's happening to me I'm not responsible for it.

You have to make a choice; no one's going to make it for you, but I tell you that the free that the freedom ends the future that you can create for yourself is limited only by your own imagination. Now you may say, how can I take control and responsibility for these things when we are being bombarded every single day with subliminal messaging from marketing from news from "the noise"?

The answer is simple once you understand the tactics and once you understand the fact that you are a target for marketing, you can begin to see it and notice it and avoid it. The scary part is once you understand How Deep The Rabbit Hole goes, you may have wished that you didn't look because it can be scary the amount of information that is collected on you and your habits and then used to promote to you. I was startled when I learned it.

Being Manipulated for Spending.

One of the biggest realizations that I came to when it concerns business and taxes was that from the government to your local news station to the Mom and Pop Shop and local Family Diner all the way to your mail, you are being manipulated for spending. This has primarily to do with our human habits and the study of our routines and tendencies so that companies can subtly influence where we spend our money.

Where this becomes startling is when you look at the amount of information that people are collecting on us and our habits on an hourly, daily, and weekly basis. You realize that they're almost isn't enough ways to quantify all of this data properly, but it's still being bought and sold all across the world. This is one of the reasons why whenever you speak about something to a friend, you'll see an ad for it on Google, you know, minutes or hours for the next day later.

I don't know how many of you have actually paid attention to that, but it's a very real thing. The level of advertising and manipulation that goes into advertising is astronomical. Let's take, for example, the abused animal videos that you see, especially during the holidays. Why do you think it is that you only see those videos around specific dates? Why is it that you think that you only see those emotionally draining, tear-jerking videos at certain times of the year? And why are they so over-the-top sappy?

It's emotional manipulation. They are trying to get you to feel pity and empathy for these animals so that you will either donate to the cause or they will spur on to some other sort of action. Now, where this comes to manipulation is because as they are creating using these ads to create an emotional response inside of you, they are then providing you with Outlets to be able to calm the response that they've created inside of you.

So they are both creating a problem of cognitive dissonance and then providing you with the solution. The action steps on what to do about it next and how to solve it which can also create a habit in your mind, one that you may already have, for example. When you're in great distress, you may very well have the response that you need to get your body out of this mode of panic. So when you become emotionally agitated or when there is conflict inside of you, it's normal human behavior to want to stop, remove that, or solve it.

So we can stop these uncomfortable feelings we can call anxiety or the fear or the pain within ourselves. If you notice in the videos, they will always tell you how you can help solve the problem, so they give you the create distress, and then they give you a pathway in which you can home field in which you can do something about it and essentially self-soothe by taking action it's really psychologically fascinating once you start digging into it and understanding human behavior, but that is a different book for a different time. How does this all link Back to two taxes and your finances?

Well, the government and the Congress and the President and politicians all do the very same thing. They want to gain control over your spending, so they incentivize you to spend in certain areas. As I've mentioned previously when laws are passed and signed by the President go into effect, most of those laws will either have a benefit to a certain sector of the economy or they will have some impact on tax legislation the general American populace and by paying attention to those markers, you will be able to figure out where the government wants you to spend.

Now the other thing that you need to keep in mind is that you can start to predict where these changes will come up based on the political campaigns of the candidates. What's taken by the administration, for example then, putting in solar or Alternative Energy tax credits into the inflation reduction Act? If you paid attention to the Democratic platform or the Biden campaign at all, read any of their policies read any of the major topics that they wanted to cover, you could have easily picked out the Alternative Energy sector as being a pet project for this administration you also have the benefit of historical data when it comes to the Biden Administration.

Let's not forget that Joe Biden was Barack Obama's vice president; what did we witness under the Obama administration? Several increases and credits, or, you know, benefits tax and legislative-wise, were given to solar companies and companies that provided options for alternative energy. Similarly, if we receive a republican candidate as president for the next election cycle and they win by paying attention to the areas of focus for the Republican party and the specific interest of that candidate, you will be able to determine the areas where they want to adjust the tax code.

Now then, the question becomes are you going to be actively participating in our legislative cycle, and you are going to be actively participating in understanding what happens when these changes come out or are you going to be passive bystanders who are manipulated by their entire life and they're spending their money their life is just out of their control, and it's something that happens to them. How you get to the point where you're in control changes your mindset. The only way you can change your mindset cuz you have to be able to change what you're feeding your mind, what's your reading, what's your listening to, what you're watching, and ultimately the people that you're associating with.

Those are the four things that you need to change in order to have an extremely successful life. Once you have that down, the next thing you need to change is the skill set you need to upgrade your skill-set so that you can be tactical in the way that you approach negotiations, sales, and ultimately, the business cycle once you're able to change your mindset and your skill set your life will change beyond recognition, and you will no longer be the person you were before, and you will have to Begin your journey the shaping yourself into the person that you want to be.

*"You're The Average of The Five People
You Spend The Most Time With".*

-Jim Rohn

CHAPTER III:
The Proof is in The Pudding

Now that you're on the journey now that you have started, hopefully on the two components of mindset and skill set to get you where you want to be in life, let's look at the specific skill sets that you're going to need when it comes to what I like to call Financial ninjutsu. Number one, you're going to have to learn how to follow the money. that is still number one; you've heard it in TV shows all the time, you've seen it in movies how do you catch the bad guys, especially when it's some Corporation or conglomerate or what have you follow the money the same thing is true when it comes to how to deal with the super-wealthy.

Did you know that every single stock trade that our Congress people make on a daily basis has to be reported? There have been so many millionaires made just by following the same trades that our civil servants do that it is ridiculous. Now I preface all of this by saying I'm not giving investment advice; I'm not saying that you should make the same trades that they make. I'm simply pointing out a fact that if you follow the money, you can figure out where the government is going to be allocating additional assets, what industries are going to be allocating funds to, and what industries are going to receive or experience a pullback.

The proof is in the pudding you have done for the last year. I have seen people on Instagram, Facebook, and Tick Tock, follow the same trading habits as Nancy Pelosi; they've gone to the website SEC.Report, and you can find all of the Congress and Senate stock trade disclosures by date time representative what have you and you can make all the same traits as well. It's crazy, but you have to follow the money. Why wouldn't you if you knew that people make it their job to influence the economy and influence specifically certain sectors of it?

If you knew where they were investing, wouldn't you want to invest along with them? If you knew that they were pulling out of a certain area or a certain company or a certain type of stock, wouldn't you also want to pull out of it? This is how you stay ahead of Trends and occurrences by paying attention, but the problem is that most of us have conned ourselves into the thoughts that we don't have enough time be able to pay attention to these things along with all the other things that we have to do every day.

Let me assure you that you have time; we all have the time. How many hours do you spend watching a mind-numbing amount of TV when you could be better in your life and bettering your children's lives, and bettering your future? But instead, you sit on your ass and complain about how life isn't going your way instead of doing something about it. Don't be that guy; don't be that person who grabs life by the horns; it's too short not to. Have you heard that saying the proof is in the pudding?

If your life isn't where you want it to be, then the proof is in the pudding, my friend your outcome is a direct representation of your input and the decisions that you've made; now we're about getting you out of that; let's follow the money let's figure out what the wealthy are doing and let's play the game you've got this let's go!

Follow the Money

Going to the SEC to follow those reports is not the only way you can follow the money there are many other ways the crazy thing is that rich people are constantly telling us how they became rich they are screaming at the top of their lungs we want you to be rich too. The only factor that remains as you are going to listen, you are going to follow the money. Are you going to do what the wealth you're doing? Are you going to listen to them? Watch what they do, not just listen to what they say.

THE IRS – Dirty Little Secrets

Now, this is an important one I want to caution you about right now; it took me a long time to figure this out, but finally, it clicked; if you listen to Gary Vaynerchuk at certain points, he will tell you to stop listening to what I say and watch what I do, and that's how you will attain what you want the same can be said about Grant Cardone the same can be said about Robert Kiyosaki the same can be said about Tony Robbins the same can be said about Brad Lea.

All of these significantly influential and successful people all have one thing in common they are doing something that they aren't particularly telling you about, but they are doing it openly and even to the point where they're telling you, hey, watch what I'm doing stop listening to what I'm saying you're consuming my content.

You're acting like a consumer; wake up, watch what I do what I'm doing, and you will be successful. The one thing that I always like to hear when I'm listening to Grant Cardone is That Money Follows attention. He's extremely famous for saying that it's been a fact in his business. Now, if you look at the trajectory in the content of his business, the content hasn't changed that much. Grant Cardone is still who Grant Cardone it's who he's always been.

He's a good salesman, he's a teacher, he's a real estate professional, an entrepreneur, and an investor, and he likes helping people. That's who he is, but if you watch what he does instead of just consuming his content, this is where and how Grant Cardone has become successful, why he was able to be on the second season of an undercover billionaire on the Discovery Channel why he has books that have gone a New York Times bestseller. Once you understand that if you Garner attention and you get people content that they can consume some of their money inevitably will follow.

If you put yourself in front of people, even if they don't like you often enough, they will come to like you over time. This is one of the quickest ways to attain wealth and success in our society currently. But there are other ways you have to know how the wealthy use money and use debt and the practices that they put in place in order to be successful and Wealthy like they are wealthy. There's a difference between being financially comfortable, being financially free, and ultimately being super wealthy. Let's break down the different components in those three sectors really quickly.

The Financially Comfortable

What does it mean to be financially comfortable? Who are the financially comfortable? And is this an area that you want to attain in your life? In this section, we're going to cover all of those questions and answer them.

To know what it means to be financially comfortable, you have to understand first the type of person that seeks financial comfort. In general, in my experience, this has been someone who has come from a middle-class family or lower-middle-class family, someone who does not have large dreams or aspirations, someone who struggles to figure out what they want to do with themselves and ultimately, at the end of the day they really just want to do their job come home and live their life.

There's nothing wrong with that; to some people, that would be a dream come true, and I will never belittle anyone's dreams; the simple fact of the matter is there just not mine. What does it mean to be financially comfortable? Well, someone that's financially comfortable makes enough money at their one job to be able to or maybe two jobs to be able to pay their bills, cover all their expenses and have a little bit left over the play with.

They have a nice work-life balance where they work a decent amount, but they still have 1, 2, or 3 days off during the week so that they can hang out with family, spend time with friends, and they'll probably have to 3 to 4 weeks of vacation every single year. This is the middle class; they may want more out of life they may not like their job, but the problem with being stuck in this section is that you're so comfortable that there's no great inspiration for change and going outside of this comfortability seems so incredibly risky that it's just unthinkable.

It's important to note that this is where the majority of the naysayers exist. When someone is starting a new business, the "be careful" speeches come from the people who maybe aren't necessarily happy with their job but make too much money to leave. Sure they make a decent wage, and to put that in Jeopardy would threaten their entire way of life, and that's not something that they are ever willing to risk. There's nothing wrong with that.

It's a very common way of life that many people choose, but there's more out there. At first, it may be incredibly scary and uncomfortable, but I promise you investing in yourself and expanding your mind will benefit you, so just to recap generally the financially comfortable come from mid to upper middle class what does it mean to be financially comfortable you have enough money to sustain your lifestyle and a little bit to do some fun things in your life, but this is your life it will be constant it will be steady, and it will be monotonous until the time that you are granted retirement, if you are ever granted retirement. Keep in mind this is not a bad place to live. It is a good life, good people come from here, but if you are trying to provide for Generations after you, this is not the place you want to end up. However, it is a good place to start.

The Financially Free

These are the people of Dave Ramsey; these are the people who want enough financial education so that they can pay off the mountain of debt they were conned into purchasing and be able to retire comfortably sooner rather than later. These are also the people that are technically in the upper middle class; they have more than enough; they go on great vacations every year, but they work a little too hard and don't get to spend enough time where they would like to.

For most of us, financially free is the goal. You've got a large 401K, you've got a nice house, you've got the picket fence, you drive a nice car, you've got money in the bank, you maybe have a couple of investment properties you have a summer home, and you're definitely not struggling to make ends meet. Your kids will probably have a college fund, and they will be set up for when they become young adults and go out on their own.

For most of us, this is the dream. It's also a trap; there are tons of people in this section that would be considered Wealthy by most of us, except most of that wealth is just on paper. They own everything. They're responsible for so much, their taxes are astronautical, and most of them just think that they're supposed to pay it. For example, everyone wants to marry a doctor, right? They make great money which, yeah, they also pay a lot of money in taxes. If you're a doctor and you make, you know High six-figure salary, you're going to be paying six figures in taxes too.

It's ridiculous most people don't understand that there's a way to go about this and that you can literally get that money back, but that's because they fall into this financially free category. They're still not playing the game that the super-wealthy are playing. They still don't know they know some of the tips and tricks some of them they've been able to increase their income above their expenses, they're able to save a little, they're able to have an elevated lifestyle, but they still don't understand everything about the game that the super wealthy do and how to play it. They think that ownership is what creates wealth, so they try to buy everything they can; they try to buy multiple cars; they try to buy multiple homes; they try to buy investments in real estate, and they don't realize at the same time, that they're opening themselves and all of their assets and their family, to the greatest liability that there is. They don't necessarily realize that they could be sued and lose everything they own, or they could become ill and lose their Financial Security. They may be free, but they're still beholden to a Master and that Master is time and health.

What Do the Super Wealthy Know and Practice?
The biggest difference between the financially comfortable and financially free and the super-wealthy is the LIE of ownership. This lie of ownership is created primarily by people that want to sell you something the real way to minimize your tax liability so that you're not responsible for it is to control everything but own nothing. This is how you attain what I call Financial Ninjutsu and become a master of your life, your finances, and your destiny.

At some point, I will probably write a book about financial ninjutsu and the factors that can be played out, and how to become a master of this delicate art. Now, what does it mean to control everything but own nothing? To most of you that's probably a very confusing statement. It's done through entities I will mention later on in Chapter 5. I'll be going into the proper structures, and the benefits for each structure taxation lies. Not going to get into that now, but what I am going to talk about is trust ownership. When you create an irrevocable living trust, that means that it is an entity one of itself...like its very own person.

This is true for any Corporation or company setup that you undertake now. Some of them are passed through, which means their profits and things are passed through to the owners directly, and others have barriers where they are taxed as if they were individuals. As an example, they have a flat or sliding-scale tax rate, or they are exempt. One of the best examples I can give of "control of everything but owning nothing" is let's say that you inherit a home from your grandfather; the home is completely paid off, there's no mortgage and the house has been kept up well over the years, so the only thing that you have to pay Is property taxes.

When you inherit this property after your grandfather passes away, you could be hit with something called an inheritance tax if it does not pass through to you properly or if there are other things in the works like large sums of life insurance or a lot of retirement accounts that exceed the amount of his lifetime gift. If you don't know what a lifetime gift is, you need to look it up. It's essentially the amount of money that one person can give another person without tax consequences in their lifetime. This can be done every single year. I say, for argument's sake, the amount of money left to you by your grandfather exceeds the amount that you can get in a lifetime, which means you'll be taxed on it.

There have been people who have had to sell a family home or estate because of this very situation, and it could have been avoided with just a little bit of planning. Now let's talk about how one of the greatest ways to transfer wealth between Generations is with a Trust. What you do is with your wealth, you transfer ownership of all your assets, especially cash flow generating assets, into the Trust so that way the Trust owns everything. Then you can maintain control of everything by naming yourself the executor of the Trust. This means you can control the funds however you like.

There are certain things that a Trust cannot spend money on, but there are very few. This is an exact example of "controlling everything and owning nothing" because now you have zero tax liability as an individual. What if you owned a multimillion-dollar business? You would have to pay profit on that every single year. When you transfer that business into the Trust, the Trust is now the owner. The Trust would be taxed on any income, but the business would pay those taxes. Quite simply, those taxes become an expense for doing business. You still control the business because you control the Trust. The only time you can be taxed is when you take money out of the Trust for personal reasons and expenses or when the trust generates taxable income. This is one of the strategies that the super wealthy use to protect assets and to get things out of their personal name, so that on paper, generally, they look broke, but they all drive nice cars and live in nice homes.

The other thing that the super wealthy do to maintain their wealth is they leverage debt, and specifically, they leverage debt on assets. Let's use the example of your grandfather's house again. It's paid off, there's no mortgage on it, you have someone coming to appraise it, and it appraises for 2.3 million dollars. You can take the equity out of that home on a home equity line of credit. Maybe it's only 1.8 million dollars because it's 80% of the home value, and you can take those 1.8 million dollars and use it however you please. That's not a taxable event. You cannot be taxed on the 1.8 million dollars because it's not income, it's debt. Your leveraging debt to buy more assets and the only thing you have to do is use that 1.8 million dollars Define an asset and buy it and cash flow enough to pay for that 1.8 million dollars. Or let's say you rent out your grandfather's home to a short-term rental or just a standard rental property.

By doing that, you could have the rent received from that property go back to pay off the 1.8 million dollars, and then every time the debt continues to be paid off, you can pull money back out; it's a remarkable, remarkable thing and that's why real estate is one of the few sectors that has made the most millionaires in America over time. You have to be able to know what the wealthy know and be able to put it into practice if you want to be ultimately successful.

Financial Ninjitsu
Now let's talk about financial ninjutsu. I've mentioned it a couple of times in previous sections, but I really want to get into what this process is, what I mean by this term, and how you can become a master in your own right. The way that I think about business is unique, but it's also very strategic, and that's why this term really resonates with me.

Not only because I happen to be a massive anime nerd but also because dealing with finances, especially creatively, and when it comes to the tax code, you have to have some skill, finesse, and agility; otherwise, you're going to get knocked flat on your ass. Wonder stands the meaning of financial ninjutsu. You must understand what ninjutsu is. Ninjutsu is essentially the modern martial art strategy and tactics of unconventional warfare, guerrilla warfare, in espionage that used to be practiced by the Ninja.

The Ninja was masterful in all of these areas, conventional warfare, guerrilla warfare, and espionage. Now, what I mean when I say Financial Ninjutsu is very much the same as becoming a financial master. One of the biggest questions that I get is what does Warfare and Espionage have to do with finances, and the truth is not much except when it comes to a strategy that's why you hear of so many people who have become successful after reading The Art of War.

This is why being tactical and having skills with your finances or putting the proper people in place that have the skill that you are lacking can be vital to your success. You don't have to be the master, but you do have to be humble and not take direction and learn from one. So, let's go over the four main principles of Financial Ninjutsu and what they look like:

Number One: Attain the based level of Financial Intelligence (learn to balance a checkbook). You have to be able to understand basic financial principles, such as a system of checks and balances or debits and credits. You also have to be able to identify what is a liability and what is an asset. Once you master these two functions, you will have a basic understanding for how money and accounting work which is ultimately the basis for the tax code.

Number Two: Gain control through your budget (You need to learn some discipline). You need to be honorable to your word, to yourself and to your money and how it's spent. To do that, you need to tell your money where to go and how it will be spent so that you aren't tossed and swayed by the manipulation of marketing that happens and that we are bombarded with every single day. This is where budgeting comes in; everyone hates to budget. Budgeting is often not seen as a fun activity because, for most people, it's more fun to just fly by the seat of your pants and not have to be responsible for something that you know you're not going to keep up anyways, so why bother to do it. Get some freaking discipline, man up or woman up, and do it. Be responsible to yourself Respect yourself enough to keep your promise to yourself, and ultimately control your financials. This is not just about personal budgeting; this also goes to business budgeting.

Number Three: Tailor your life so that it is in line with your business or side hustle. Make your personal life almost indistinguishable from your business. If you can do this, then everything that you do becomes a business expense and is generally tax deductible. A lot of people are scared to do this because they're like, "Oh my God, what if I get audited by the IRS?" First of all, as long as you're not doing anything illegal, there should be no fear of having the IRS look at what you're doing. Secondly, as long as you have a proper paper trail for everything that you do and every dollar that you spend, you will never have to worry about it. This is one of the three foundational principles of financial ninjutsu. The reason this is so pivotal is that this is the very embodiment of leveraging the tax code to your benefit.

Number Four: Assemble your team of advisors. Build a team around your life and your business of like-minded advisors that have attained the same or greater things than you have so far in your life. When you surround yourself with people that have achieved the same level of success that you have or preferably a greater level of success, you can then garner from that experience and from those advisors the steps to take your business to the next level. The collective knowledge and experience of other people and utilizing that collective experience and knowledge can give you the best advantage both in life and in business. This is where leverage comes into play. Learning to avoid the pitfalls that others have experienced before you and adding your own experience to their lives can lead to an incredible level of fulfillment.

These are the four foundational principles for financial ninjutsu. Learning to add these basic building blocks to your life and your entrepreneurial journey will cut out years of pain and can catapult you and the other people in your circle to new levels and new heights of success.

> *"What you get by achieving your goals is not as important as what you become by achieving your goals."*
>
> -Zig Ziglar

CHAPTER IV:
When You Know Better-You Do Better

You may have heard the old adage that knowledge is power. In certain circumstances, that is most definitely true; however, I would strongly argue that knowledge itself is not power, but rather applied knowledge is power. The knowledge itself does not give you anything more than the capacity to do great things, and to use that knowledge is actually the application of that knowledge and the working out in day-to-day activities that gives the knowledge width and breadth.

I understand how knowledge can be transformed through practical application to power. You have to understand in what forms the power will manifest. There are many people in this world that have a lot of book knowledge, and there are many people in this world that have practical knowledge. Where this principle becomes most powerful is when those two intersect, and your intellectual knowledge and your practical knowledge lead to applicable and trackable results. There are many different ways to quantify results, but two of the most poignant ends to be through is money and respect.

Knowledge is Power Manifesting in Money and Respect
For a lot of people like myself who struggled with Traditional School, there was a constant reinforcement that we were going to struggle in the real world. Generally, this bias comes from the fact that we did not fit the standard mold; we were too loud, too excitable, too energetic, and most of all, too hard to control. This is where the common Parable comes into play when you hear people talk about that C and D students becoming the employers of the A and B students.

I don't know if you have ever heard that before, but it was something that actually became very true in my personal life. When we were talking about applied knowledge being power, we need to understand what that power will manifest as because, for a lot of people I know, for me, it was never clearly defined. I was always left wondering, well, what good will this applied knowledge be? How will I know when I've made it? How will I know when I have become successful? How will I know when I have gained any sort of power in this world?

One of the ways that power from knowledge manifests is through monetary gain and respect from others. This can be a very slippery slope because a lot of people seek to gain the approval of those around them. That's not what I'm talking about. I'm not talking about respect as in approval of those around you or of your parents or of your spouse or your friends or your family. The kind of respect that I'm talking about is when there is a problem that someone needs solved, and they call you because they know you have the knowledge to solve their problem and make their life better.

That is a level of respect that can transcend any of your shortcomings that you may have struggled with seeking approval in your past. Unfortunately, some of those people that you have always sought approval from in your past could benefit most from the applied knowledge that you have, but because they are constantly living with an old dead version of whom you used to be in their mind, they will never humble themselves to reach out to you and gain from the knowledge that you possess. Even if it is the very thing that could change their life for the better. one of the main things that you need to realize and you can come to terms with is that, that is okay.

It is not your responsibility to save them as much as you wish you could. Now once we have this applied knowledge and we know how to use it to get results, let's talk about how the manifestation of that power is gained.

Money Follows Attention

Grant Cardone talks about this all the time; it's one of the pivotal points that he talks about in marketing all the time, and I've mentioned it a couple of times already. The fact that money follows attention. You can have the greatest knowledge in the world, and have been able to apply that knowledge in many situations; and achieved results and outcomes better than you ever expected for yourself and those you have already helped. But how is anyone going to know that you have this wealth of information and experience and the solution to their problems if they don't know anything about you or even Who You Are?

The short answer is they can't benefit from it if they don't know you. You need to demonstrate that applied knowledge. You need to get your message out there, and you need to start creating content to do so. If money follows attention in this day and age, how do we get attention? You have to be willing to look stupid, and you have to be willing to be unprofessional for a time, and you have to be willing to put the information and yourself out there because there's no point in being the world's best-kept secret.

You will drive yourself to financial ruin, you will always be operating from a scarcity mindset, and you will never be able to have enough if you don't get people to know who you are. This is not a marketing book. Marketing is a core asset in business. You need to learn how to promote yourself. You need to learn how to develop a brand, and you need to learn how to connect with the people that you have the skill set and the power to help. By not doing so and refusing to market yourself, you are actually being selfish. A lot of people have trouble with this because of fear or because they're a perfectionist.

They don't want to put out a product that they're not proud of, even if that product is a video or a post on social. If you're just starting out in business, there are several things that you can do aside from social media. Use ads to get your message out, connect with people, and provide value to the marketplace. One of the best ways to do this is to get involved in your local community. Getting involved in a Chamber of Commerce, getting involved in a local Business Association, finding out who your ideal customer is and going to them and the places that they go, and adding value there.

Doing this without expecting a return or a sale will separate you from the already established competitors in the market. When it boils down to it, people do business with people that they like, that they know, and whom they trust. To become those three things, you need to get out there and get amongst the people. It may be scary at first; you may not know how to identify the people that you're looking for, and you may not even know how to help them get what they want so that you can provide your resources to them in the future. Brad Lea once told me That if you can build a community of people around you and help them achieve their goals, then that community of people should not let you struggle financially.

If they are not also supporting your business like you're supporting their business and their goals and their dreams, then it's time to get around some new people. Zig Ziglar was once quoted that, "You will get all you want in life if you help enough other people get what they want in life." that could not be more true. I strongly suggest that if you want to learn how to market yourself and garner attention to become massively successful, watch what Grant Cardone does and how often he posts on social media. See and watch how often Gary Vaynerchuk posts on social media. Watch how often Brad Lea post on social media, and go out and mimic their posts.

Don't just mimic their posts; mimic how often they are posting; go to their pages and set your social pages up to look similar to theirs. Obviously, you are going to have different content; you're not an expert necessarily in what they are experts in, but here's the thing; structure, the format, and the type of copy that they are posting are what you need to mimic. The reason for that is that it's already proven to be successful it works for them; it's what got them to the level that they are at. And once you've begun to gain notoriety once you have begun to gain a foothold in your local community, you can then expand that community online and beyond.

Once you do that, people will come to you for their needs; people will come to you if they know what you are selling and what you have, and the value you add to the marketplace people will come to you. You don't have to live in scarcity, scraping by barely being able to have enough. The reason that you are dealing with this scarcity is that not enough people know what you can do and who you are, and the value that you can add to their lives. Grant Cardone says it best, "best-known beats the best product every time."

Respect Follows Integrity
Now that we've talked about how money follows attention and the steps you need to take to get attention, especially when you're starting out, let's talk about respect and integrity. Once you've gone through the business cycle, you come up with your idea you've created an offering for what that product or service solves for the market. Now you need to bring your product or service to market.

This is where integrity comes into play. Unfortunately, in business, it takes all kinds of people in our world to make up the free market. There are unethical people out there, there are bad companies out there, and there are people that will take advantage of you, but none of those people ever stay in business for generations. They oftentimes don't even stay in business for years. If you do not operate your business with integrity, you will never gain respect. If you want to create a legacy. If you want to create long-term wealth where you can take care of the generation that came before you and the generations that come after you, then you must operate your business and organize your life around integrity.

Now, what is integrity? I've heard it best in a religious context, especially in the Bible - Matthew 5:37; the verse is simple, yet sweet "But let your yes be yes and your no be no. for anything more comes from the evil one". This principle is especially true in business; if you say that you're going to do something, you had better damn well do it, and if you say no to something, you need to understand what you're saying no to, and you need to stand firm on that and have the integrity to do so.

To me, this is the exemplification have integrity itself. If you can operate your business at this level of integrity and simply just keep your word, be honest with your product or service and do your best to try and help people achieve their goals, dreams, and desires, then you will be respected in your community you will be respected in your profession you will be respected at someone that they can come to with a need and they can trust you to solve their problem. Establishing this in your business is the best way to create long-term generational wealth. This should be the cornerstone of how you operate and conduct yourself in business. This is why respect it's the by-products of integrity.

This is also why long-term wealth and generational wealth are the by-products of respect and integrity. If you can manage to gain enough attention where people know you, they see you, they like you, and they trust you and then operate at a high level of integrity, you will never want for anything, and generations after. You will reap the rewards of your success and integrity.

> *"Clients, employees, family, friends, whoever is holding you back from meeting your dreams... DROP THEM."*
>
> *-Andrew Argue, CPA*

CHAPTER V:
Structure is Key

We have talked a lot in previous chapters, specifically about mindset and the building blocks for taking advantage of everything contained in the tax code. We've also discussed a lot of the things necessary to maintain longevity in business. Now let's get into the structure of how business entities are formed and when it is applicable to utilize these structure types to you get the most benefit from the tax code.

There are five basic types of entity structure; there are sole Proprietors, LLCs, Partnerships, S-Corps, and C-Corps. Each of these structure types has its own benefits, and even in certain instances when they are layered in combination with other entities, even entities of the same type, they can provide substantial asset protection and protection from increased tax liability. If these are not put into place properly, the opposite outcome can still happen if you do not have the right entity structure in place. You can actually end up overpaying taxes which is where the majority of American entrepreneurs are currently at today.

Many people could benefit from significant tax savings simply by implementing the correct entity structure. I'm going to go over each entity structure and give you a base overview So that you can understand when these entities' structures should be used and when you should move on to a more appropriate entity structure.

Choosing Your Business Vehicle and Tax Benefits
The first entity structure that most people overlook and that some people don't even consider to be an actual entity structure or business structure is the sole proprietor. This structure type is the easiest to utilize, but each state varies on its requirements around setting this up. In some States, you may not be required to do anything to set up operating as a sole proprietor as long as you are using your name and your Social Security number. But a lot of people don't

realize that this affords you the same ability under the tax code to generate revenue and deduct business expenses as any formally Incorporated LLC or partnership.

Sole Proprietor
What this does not afford you is the liability protection that comes with having a formally established Corporation such as an LLC. When you do business as a Sole Proprietor, you can deduct everything that's a natural business expense that you would be able to adopt under the other Corporation types, except you do not have the ability without the registration in your state and with the IRS to have employees or to employ yourself as a W-2 employee. You can utilize all the other deductions that every other business can utilize. This is one of the simplest and most straightforward forms or entities that you can do business as.

The income you generate as a Sole Proprietor goes directly to your income as an individual minus your business or operating expenses, and then what's left over, what your net profit is, is what you are taxed on. For anyone who has a side hustle or for anyone who is just starting out in business, this is where you should start prior to earning your first revenue in business. I should also caution you that it depends on the type of business that you are conducting and what the risks are for conducting that business because, as I mentioned earlier, there is no liability protection under this entity; all of your personal assets could be the target of a lawsuit if you are in a business where you could potentially be sued.

Unfortunately, this goes for everything from Real Estate all the way to coaching and everything in between. If you can imagine that there is a risk of being sued for any reason, then you should consider incorporating into one of the other types on top of having insurance that will protect you and your personal assets, including your business, from any potential lawsuits that could occur.

LLC

The next type of entity structure is probably the most popular and one of the most referred to and preferred methods of incorporation in the US. This is the limited liability Corporation, and this entity type is first registered with your state, then registered with the IRS to get an EIN number so that you and your business and your personal assets have greater protection if there should be any liability that could arise for any lawsuit that could arise.

There are also several tax advantages to becoming an LLC. Some of those are that you can now easily register with the state to have employees as well as with the IRS, and you can opt to have this entity taxed as a different type of entity while still maintaining your LLC structure. What that means is you could be treated tax-wise as an S-Corp while still maintaining your operations and structure as an LLC. It is also important to note that owners of an LLC are called members, not partners or owners. There are also some limitations to this entity type. The limitations for this entity type are that there are several Industries that are not permitted to be in LLC, such as Banking and insurance.

Some of the other drawbacks are that this will also increase your compliance costs, as well as probably your tax preparation cost record-keeping costs oh, and would likely result in increased Administration fees to the state where you are Incorporated. Another limitation that oftentimes people don't realize is that transferring ownership of an LLC can oftentimes be harder to do than with other entity types.

For example, if you have multiple members in your LLC, which there is no limit on the number of members you can have, but unless the members agree to Add a new owner or transfer ownership to someone else and alter your operating agreement, you could run into a legal battle in order to transfer your ownership in the LLC to someone else who is not already a member. All that being said, though, it is still one of the most widely used entity types in the US, and other than the sole proprietor has one of the more straightforward taxation and is lower-cost annually, specifically with compliance than the other entity types.

It is also important to note that once you have multiple members of an LLC, you then have to file a separate tax return for the business itself. With a Sole Proprietor and a single-member LLC, those get filed with your personal tax return. This is why I often advise married couples who want to get into business together not to add both spouses to the LLC unless they are aware of how this will affect their tax preparation and potential liability at the end of the year.

Partnership
Partnerships can be a very useful entity formation, and these are often done between married couples or people that get in business for a very specific situation, project, or product. This entity type is formed similarly to the LLC and can oftentimes be referred to as an LLP, a limited liability partnership. Different states have different classifications and regulations surrounding partnerships, but for this example, we're going to be looking at what would be qualified as a joint venture.

The joint venture means that both parties are equally contributing to the formation and The Business and equally responsible for the business; this would be considered a 50/50 partnership. This is why it can be a popular formation type for married couples because if you are going 50-50 into business with one another, it can build on your other relationships, such as your marriage which you could have been doing as 50/50 already.

Now I get it. You may believe marriage should be 100%/100% from both parties and not 50/50, but for the sake of argument, let's just assume that it's 50/50. The registration process is still very similar to that. Let's see, you register with the state forming the partnership, then you register your EIN with the IRS, claiming it as a partnership, and then the IRS on your EIN letter will tell you at the end of the year what tax form this business entity needs to file.

The reason that I bring marriage into it is that if it is truly a joint venture with a married couple, you can still file the business with your personal taxes; you do not need to file a separate tax return for the business, but if your partner is not a related party, then you have to file a separate form or tax return with the IRS to make sure there's proper allocation of the business's income and expenses. A partnership, much like an LLC, Sole Proprietorship, and an S-Corp, is all that is considered by the states and the IRS pass-through entities meaning that the profit from the businesses blows through to you as the owner as self-employment income. in the next two entity types there are considerably more options for tax savings, tax strategy, and overall planning then you can actually do in a partnership LLC or Sole Proprietorship.

S-Corp
This is where we get into the meat and potatoes. An S-Corp, in general, is one of the most tax-advantaged entity types that exist currently. You have the most flexibility and the most options with this entity type than you do with almost any other. You can incorporate directly into an s-Corp; however, you can also incorporate as an LLC and then elect to file the proper paperwork with the IRS and the state where you are Incorporated to be treated as an S-Corp while still maintaining your LLC structure and members.

This is also one of the few entity types where you are allowed to be an employee of your own company. This is one thing that a lot of people overlook and do incorrectly see; one of the regulations for being taxed as an S-Corp for owning an S-Corp is that, as the owner, you must be paid a reasonable salary for the work that you do within the business. A lot of people had gotten into trouble and been audited because they did not have to pay themselves a reasonable salary from the business when they converted from an LLC to an S-Corp but still continued to take money out of business. Some of the drawbacks to an S corporation are that the shareholders must be U.S. citizens or resident aliens in order to hold ownership in the company.

You also must file a separate tax return from your personal tax return for this entity type. However, there are many benefits to owning a Scorp. one of the largest benefits is that you can give yourself a W-2 salary as well as take distributions from the company that could be tax-free. These distributions are decided on something that is called Basis. The Basis is a complicated calculation that is essential. It Tells you as an owner what your investment and stake are in the business.

This is calculated based on your initial investment into the company when it was started, any monetary or property Investments you contribute to the business during its operation, or any money that you have loaned the business to continue its operations. Your basis increases based on the revenue generated by the company throughout the year and then is decreased by any expenditures against that operating income. Once that calculation has taken place, you are then left with how much money you can take out of the business to essentially pay yourself back. One of the interesting things is that you can also take out a loan from the company as an owner or shareholder, and then that loan will stay on the books with the company until you pay it back.

There is no maturity date; there is no length of time in which these loans have to come off of the books, but when you are looking for additional funding from third parties such as Banks or venture capital, all of these things go into consideration because they will show up on the books and the reports that you provide to these third parties in consideration for Lending purposes. This entity also provides you with the greatest protection for your personal assets, as well as, gives you an opportunity to take part in retirement programs such as a 401k, defined benefit plan, or another retirement vehicle. One of the greatest powers that an S-Corp has is the ability for you to take money out of the corporation without having tax consequences. Oh, and this is also why it is one of the most tax advantage entity types there are.

Now, a Sole Proprietorship, an LLC, a Partnership, and a C Corporation can all lead to a situation called double taxation. An S-Corp is an entity type that allows you to avoid this double taxation. Double taxation usually occurs when you are taxed for income purposes, income tax on profit oh, and then also taxed on self-employment income from the business. Unfortunately, with an S-Corp, there are also increased tax preparation fees and compliance costs that go along with it which is why I usually advise companies, especially LLCs that have just started, that you do not need to convert to an S-Corp until you are making at least $100,000 a year in revenue because the compliance costs do not outweigh the tax benefits that you can receive and you may end up actually paying more then if you had just stuck with your original incorporation.

Corporation/C Corp
A corporation or C Corp is probably one of the more complicated legal tax entities that exist within the US tax

code. However, there are many significant benefits to having this type of corporation. The steps to incorporate this entity type are a little bit different, you still need to register with the state as the proper entity type, pay the filing fees, and then properly register with the IRS as the same entity type. There are some additional record-keeping and compliance steps that you need to take into account when you're setting up this type of company.

Some of those additional requirements are that you need to have a Board of Directors which can consist only of yourself, but that is not necessarily advisable. You also need to maintain regular meetings and have a record of your meeting minutes on file, and this can come in handy when there are legal proceedings, as well as should you ever be audited by the state for the IRS.

You also need to document the shareholders' and directors' corporate decisions as well as maintain separation between the corporation and the owner's officers and directors; you must keep detailed financial records, and as I say with anything else document-document-document. You will also be required to file a separate tax form for this type of entity. Now some of the benefits that you are afforded by having this type of entity is a separate legal identity, so this type of corporation is treated almost as if it were a person rather than a company as the others are treated.

There is a significant limitation in liability to the owners of this entity type, and probably one of the most attractive things is that this entity type can operate in perpetuity outside of its owners forever, which means if you were to die or if you wanted to pass this on to your children you could very easily and the company could continue to run without you and there would be no issues of ownership or the transference of ownership. Another huge benefit to this entity type is that there is a separation between ownership and management. Basically, when you have a C Corp, you have a Board of Directors, and these Board of Directors do not necessarily need to materially participate in the company themselves. This is often where we see in the movies and media references of boardrooms and things like that. There are all those people sitting around a table making decisions for how the company should run or this, that, or the other. They are operating in this entity type.

Another large benefit Is that there is no restriction on ownership. You can have foreign investors. You could have people from other countries investing in your company and buying shares, and ultimately you could be put on the stock exchange as this type of entity. This is especially helpful if you want to receive venture capital or investments from people outside of the U.S.; there is widespread acceptance of this entity type being the preference for venture capitalists and investors because they have the ability then to get income from outside sources in order to invest in US companies. You can also offer stock to employees as incentives and part of their compensation structure.

There are also many tax planning incentives around this type of entity. Another benefit is the low tax rate on income or profit generated by the corporation. The corporate tax rate in the U.S. is a flat 21%, and that is across the board. There's no increase based on the amount of income or profit that the company generates, which is not the case for individuals, especially individuals with pass-through entities such as Sole Proprietors, LLCs and S-Corps. for example, you could make 2 million dollars of profit in a C Corp and only be taxed at 21%, but if you as an individual where you have that same $2 Million taxable income, you would pay the highest tax bracket at 37% rather than the 21% that the company would be taxed at, which is a savings of about $300,000, which is a significant amount of money, especially when you're talking about giving it to the government.

No matter which entity type you are starting out as or which one you change to in the future, it's important to know all of the requirements and milestones you need to achieve in order to make changing entities a good strategic decision, specifically when it comes to taxes. As I stated previously, the vast majority of entrepreneurs and businesses are incorporated incorrectly in the U.S. to the point where it's actually hurting their taxation and costing them more money than they should be paying every year. Hopefully, this has been easily explained, and you have a deeper understanding of where you're at or where you need to be to take advantage of the savings for the type of entity that you have.

> *"The greater danger for most of us lies not in setting our aim too high and falling short; but in setting our aim too low, and achieving our mark."*
>
> *-Michelangelo*

CHAPTER VI:
Loophole Benefits

What Tax Loopholes Can You Legally Take Advantage of?

This section is probably one of my favorites; this is where I get to geek out all over tax code loopholes and the strategies that the wealthy use on a regular basis to save money on taxes. I'm going to be explaining some of the easiest strategies that you probably didn't even know existed that you could be taking advantage of right now to save you thousands every single year. But before we get into the individual strategies, let's talk about these loopholes and what they actually are.

Many people throw around the term loophole in my industry. You can say it's sort of a buzzword, but in reality, it's just portions of the tax code that reward you for using them; that's it. There's nothing illegal about tax loopholes. To be honest, they're really not even loopholes; some of them are old laws that have been on the books for years. Because so many people take advantage of them, especially our politicians, the things that people can use, but because we're not educated about them in school or anywhere else for that matter, how are we supposed to know they exist?

Do you want to be the one waiting through 26000 pages of tax code just to find out where you can save a few thousand bucks? Some of you that answer maybe yes, but for others of you, that answer is a resounding "hell no". Sometimes people wonder if taking advantage of or utilizing these quote-unquote loopholes is going to raise any red flags or make them more likely to get audited. The answer to that is no. If these strategies are executed properly, there's no increase in your likelihood of getting audited. What most people don't realize is that most audits are completely random.

One of the things that the IRS does is it will review your tax return for errors primarily in a few categories, one of them being not reporting the proper amount of income based on what was filed with the IRS and what's filed on your tax return, the next is improper use of deductions for example if you claim a home office deduction and then claim a utility deduction for a home-based business located at the same address as your home and home office you are deducting the same amount twice potentially the IRS's going to review that and question it and ask you to provide proof. These are the largest errors that most people who prepare their own taxes and inexperienced text preparers often make. These can lead to the IRS adjusting your tax return or asking you to provide proof; this is not an audit.

An audit is much more intrusive. The IRS has a higher level of involvement in it. This is simply is plain out of a system of checks and balances in order to make sure that people are utilizing and recording and reporting their taxes, income and expenses properly. So when it comes to loopholes, there's nothing illegal about them; they are contained in the tax code. They are legal to use, and you simply just have to know how to implement them properly yourself or have a professional that has experience utilizing them and they can implement them properly on your behalf and advise you on the proper records that you need to keep in order to support these deductions. That's enough about that. Let's get into the fun stuff.

Augusta Loophole
One of my favorite tax loopholes is called the Augusta rule. Essentially this portion of the tax code was written based on the need that surrounded the Augusta, Georgia Golf Tournament that happens every year. This allows business owners to essentially rent their home to their business for up to 14 calendar days in a tax year Without having to claim that money received from the business for rent as income. Oh, this also allows the business to take a deduction for rent and corporate events, and as long as it is

under 14 days in a tax year and you do not have to claim your home as a rental property.

There is a lot that goes into this; some research to find out what the average meeting space or party rental space goes for in your area, and then make sure that you do not exceed 14 days. To do this properly, you should have contracts in place between the business and yourself dictating the terms of the rental, the price etc. But if done properly, this allows you to take money out of business tax-free as well as additional claim expenses on the business. This is probably one of the most underutilized loopholes that's currently on the books. One of the reasons for that is that a lot of people tend to feel guilty for taking money out of business and not having to pay tax on it.

Hopefully, if you're reading this book, you are not one that suffers from such an affliction. This is a great addition to any tax strategy that you currently have in place, and if you're not currently doing it and you have a business, this could save you hundreds of dollars every single year as well as give your business a local way to celebrate its employees or your clients or customers in your very own home. as with any tax strategy or deduction documentation is key and maintaining proper documentation surrounding this loophole is key.

Self Employed Health Insurance Credit
As a self-employed individual or business owner, you may be eligible for a tax credit for health insurance premiums under the Affordable Care Act (ACA). This tax credit can help offset the cost of health insurance and make it more affordable for those who are self-employed or own a small business.

To qualify for the tax credit, you must be self-employed or own a small business with fewer than 25 full-time equivalent employees (FTEs), and you must pay at least half of your employee's health insurance premiums. The credit is calculated based on the number of FTEs and the average annual wages of those employees.

To claim the tax credit, you must purchase health insurance through the Small Business Health Options Program (SHOP) Marketplace. This is an online marketplace where small businesses and self-employed individuals can shop for and compare health insurance plans.

Once enrolled in a plan through the SHOP Marketplace, you can claim the tax credit on your annual tax return. The credit is calculated as a percentage of the premiums paid for the health insurance plan, with the percentage increasing as the number of FTEs and average annual wages decrease.

In addition to the tax credit, the ACA also includes several other provisions that can benefit self-employed individuals and business owners. These include the ability to purchase health insurance without being subject to pre-existing condition exclusions and the requirement that health insurance plans cover certain essential health benefits.

Overall, the self-employed health insurance tax credit can be a valuable tax strategy for self-employed individuals and business owners. By taking advantage of this credit, you can offset the cost of health insurance and save money on your taxes. It's important to carefully review the eligibility requirements and learn how to claim the credit in order to maximize your savings.

Bonus Depreciation and Section 179 Deductions
As a business owner, it is important to understand the various tax strategies that are available to you. Two such strategies are bonus depreciation and Section 179

deductions, which can provide significant tax savings for businesses that qualify.

Bonus depreciation allows businesses to claim an additional depreciation deduction for qualified property. This property includes new assets such as buildings, machinery, vehicles, and equipment. The additional deduction of up to 100% of the cost of the property allows businesses to write off a larger portion of the cost in the year it is placed in service.

Section 179 deductions, on the other hand, allow businesses to write off the full cost of qualifying property in the year it is placed in service. This property includes tangible assets such as machinery, equipment, and certain software. Unlike bonus depreciation, which is limited to a new property, Section 179 deductions can be applied to both new and used properties.

Both bonus depreciation and Section 179 deductions can provide significant tax savings for the self-employed and businesses. They allow you to write off a larger portion of the cost of their property in the year it is placed in service rather than having to spread the deductions out over several years through regular depreciation. This can provide businesses with a much-needed cash infusion and help them invest in growth.

However, there are some limitations to both bonus depreciation and Section 179 deductions. For example, bonus depreciation is only available for a new property, and the amount of the additional depreciation deduction may be limited depending on the type of property and when it was placed in service.

One such example of this bonus depreciation loophole is with vehicles over 6000 pounds. If you purchase a vehicle that is over 6,000 lb, you can take bonus depreciation of about 100% of the value of that vehicle the year it is placed in service. What makes this interesting is the fact that you don't need to purchase the vehicle outright with cash; you can finance the purchase price of the vehicle and still take a 100% bonus depreciation deduction on the entire amount financed or the entire purchase price of the vehicle. This can be a good stop gap at the end of the year if you have unanticipated profits that you do not want to be taxed.

Section 179 deductions are also subject to limitations. The amount of the deduction is limited to a certain amount each year, and it phases out at higher levels of property purchases. Additionally, certain types of property, such as real estate, are not eligible for the deduction.

In order to take advantage of bonus depreciation and Section 179 deductions, it is important to understand the qualifications and limitations of each. It is also advisable to consult with your tax professional to determine if these strategies are right for your business.

"People Don't Recognize Opportunity, because it looks like Risk."

-Brad Lea

CHAPTER VII:
Evasion Versus Avoidance

Many people hate paying taxes to the government and to the IRS; however, an equal amount of people are terrified not to pay taxes to the IRS. They feel obligated that they must pay for fear of what could happen to them. If you have ever felt that way, let me take this moment to first apologize, but you've been made to feel that way, and let me assure you that while if you have a taxable income, you should be taxed on that money but far too many people have been overpaying in taxes needlessly for years without ever knowing that there was a better way.

Without being told that they had the power to utilize the tax code to their benefit, not just let taxes happen to them. There's always debate around whether it is wrong or right to pay taxes, and oftentimes we hear politicians spouting nonsense about people paying their fair share. The truth of the matter is that everyone under the law is required to pay their fair share, and you will pay your fair share regardless of whether you leverage the law to your benefit or you allow the law to be used against you to your detriment. When it comes to taxes, there is nothing about morality; it's not about right or wrong, it's about education, and hopefully, in the course of this book, you will be able to change your mindset on how you view taxes and how you view income and how you view entrepreneurship.

It's my goal to educate as many people as possible about the fact that you have been fed bad information for your entire life concerning finances, money, and most of all, taxes. We often hear the old saying that there are only two things to be sure of in life, one being dead; oh, and the other being taxes. Let me take a moment right now to tell you that taxes are not a sure thing. They change every single year, sometimes in small ways, sometimes in big ways, but it's important to understand the impact that the politicians we elect have on our taxes and where our money is going and how we are responsible for upholding the law and taking advantage of everything that we are able to.

Then we are also responsible for taking this knowledge and passing it on, so please, if this book so far has inspired you, share that inspiration with others, whether it be through personal education or by passing along this book. One of the main points that I want to get through to everyone who reads this is that there is a huge difference between doing something illegal like tax evasion and leveraging the tax code to your benefit so that you avoid paying taxes that you aren't supposed to be paying. You ultimately are the architect of your own life, oh, your own destiny. Likewise, you are also responsible for how much you pay in taxes.

Many times people say that the super wealthy own nothing and control everything, that's sort of a misnomer because ownership happens at some point, but it's the way that they choose to operate and control these assets that they own through other vehicles rather than owning them outright themselves. There's a very clear difference between evasion and avoidance, and tax evasion generally looks like lying about your income, whether it is not declaring cash has income, whether it is lowering the amount of income that you have received through your business or other means and not reporting that to the IRS or at least not reporting it properly oh, but it can also look like inflating your expenses so that you are reducing wrongfully the amount of money that you were showing a profit. That is tax evasion in a nutshell, and it is a crime; it is illegal, and you should not work with anyone that promotes that type of behavior because it will eventually lead you to consequences.

Let us not forget that all of the untouchable criminals, whether it be the mafia or others, when the government could not get them on a crime, were always able to find a way to get them on tax evasion in order to put them behind bars doesn't make those same mistakes. Let's talk about tax avoidance; there is nothing wrong with avoiding paying taxes; you can do so very legally; to be able to legitimately avoid paying needless taxes, you need to have an understanding of the tax law and the loopholes, some of which we've covered already in this book that you can utilize to your benefit and that the law was written for you to utilize.

When it comes to lowering your tax liability and avoiding overpayments to the government, you are actually operating in the way that the law was designed to work. I can't find anything personally wrong with that; in fact, to me, it's more wrong to overpay the government because you only have three years in which you can go back to get that money back from the IRS. to me that is more wrong losing the money that you have worked so hard for and that you could have saved had you known better, that is far more wrong in my opinion then leveraging the tax code to work in your benefit and designing your life in your business in such a way that it takes full advantage of those opportunities letter written in the law for your specific benefit.

Taxes Are Mandatory When You Don't Spend Correctly
One of the common falsehoods that I hear people talk about all the time is that taxes are mandatory, especially when they're starting a new business. I will hear people say all the time I here that I have to make quarterly payments, or if I start a business, I'm going to have to make quarterly payments. The truth of the matter is that it is a bald-faced lie; you do not have to make quarterly payments unless you do not pay the proper amount that you end up owing. And oftentimes, especially when a business is just starting out, the reason that you would end up owing any money at all it's because you are not spending your money appropriately in the business.

What do I mean by that? Well, it's very simple the IRS classifies a business deduction as anything that is an ordinary and necessary cost incurred to operate your business. This is a very broad definition, and so many things fall under this category that it is very easy to rationalize spending in your business as a business expense. These business expenses Can be travel they can be meals they could be rental cars these expenses could be office supplies such as paper, pencils, pens, and printer ink, and it could be fees that you pay two people to help you do your business, whether they be employees or contractors. It could also be wages that you pay yourself as an employee of the business can also contribute to your retirement and claim it as a deduction.

It could be promotional items, as people like to say these days merch. The possibilities are astronomical, and if you can learn to live your life within the confines of your business, you can live a TailorMade lifestyle of your own design and choosing. This is the freedom of Entrepreneurship that is made specifically possible by leveraging the tax code properly and learning how to spend your money in your business according to this tax code. Once you learn how to spend your money appropriately, you can do anything. You could go to masterminds all around the world, network with other entrepreneurs doing business remotely, traveling seeing places you had only dreamed about while you're operating your business, and the business will fund these trips as long as they are not personal in nature.

You could drive the car of your dreams and purchase it through your business, using it to conduct business on a regular basis. This means that it is now a business expense for you to own that vehicle. The same thing goes with homes; you could be a real estate investor who owned homes or properties all around the world and have the ability to utilize these homes personally when they're not being rented out or used for other business purposes, and as a natural course of business you will get to stay in these homes visit these places all while working towards your business goals and learning to customize your lifestyle.

As with anything, there's always a fine line between using the tax code and abusing the tax code, and it's a fine line to walk, which is why you need a group of advisors around you that can make sure you're operating within the confines of the law. This is primarily why I called this book The IRS's Dirty Little Secret because the secret is that the tax code overwhelmingly benefits entrepreneurs because that is where the government wants us to invest all of the money that we save on taxes. As entrepreneurs the government makes up for it in other ways that is the beauty of the tax code. You don't have to feel like you're doing anything wrong by leveraging it to your benefit because there are internal checks and balances put into place to where the government will always get their pound of flesh.

They will always get what is owed to them because of the law but the level of freedom and customizability you have available to you, your lifestyle by learning how to leverage the tax code and use it properly, and most of all, by learning how to spend your money, use your money properly so that it works for you instead of you working only for it, can and will take you to places that you have only dreamed of. Once you grasp this concept, you will truly realize that you are only limited by your own imagination. That is why every successful entrepreneur that tries to help other people become successful. It is always mindset first, then skill set, and there's a good reason for it because if you cannot envision the life you want to live, if you cannot see yourself doing it and living that life in your mind, you will not be able to achieve it.

Outside of learning how to spend your money properly and making it work for you; instead of you working for it, you have to ask yourself the question who is going to do more good with your money, the IRS? Our government? Or you, yourself, the individual, labored to earn that money? Hands down, your money is always better in your pocket than in the government. The reason for this is that the impact of a single hand holding another single hand from across the globe and never be duplicated by an institution. This is why personal responsibility and personal responsibility for one another are vital.

When we give our tax dollars to the government and expect them to take care of people that we can't be bothered to take care of ourselves, it removes the responsibility of us caring for one another. Entrepreneurship stands in direct defiance. Did this mode of operation, entrepreneurs can be some of the most generous people in the world comment, but they are still people, and some can be the most selfish in the world.

These are oftentimes the people that become the stories we use to warn other people against their behavior, or they become people that will never be remembered in this world because the impact that they left behind was not a bright spot in a dark world, rather they added to the darkness that was already here. As an entrepreneur and a business owner, you have a responsibility to take care of the people and employees in your charge; you have a responsibility to take care of your clients; you have a responsibility to care for your community; imagine how much richer all of our communities would be if we started leveraging the tax code to our own benefit as it is written and kept the money in our communities uplifting and supporting each other both emotionally and financially as well as spiritually. You can take this as a challenge to be the best thing that has happened to your family and your community by being that hand that reaches across the table to touch another living soul.

"The Purpose of Success is to create opportunity for others, it's up to them what they do with it."

-Grant Cardone

CHAPTER VIII:
Do Not Perish for Lack of Knowledge

Firstly, I would like to congratulate you for making it this far. Hopefully, by now, you've started to understand the mindset and some of the practical tools that you have in your tool belt because of the tax code and how it's written in the secrets, oh, that is not so Secret, contained within it. I hope you have begun to look at life and your reality just a bit differently so that you can truly capture what it is you want out of life so that generations that come after you will be blessed by the decisions and the actions, and the steps you take to educate yourself and those around you from this point forward.

There's a verse in the Bible, specifically, that talks about my people perishing for lack of vision. This comes from one of my favorite books of the Bible, Proverbs. The full verse comes from Proverbs 29: 18. In states, "where there is no vision, the people perish, but he that keepeth the law happy is he." This is from the King James version. This one verse can probably encapsulate everything that I've been trying to communicate to you through this book. But I would add one thing to this you can also perish from a lack of knowledge. that is why I continually talk about mindset.

A great man named Bill Britt once said, "I would rather have my mind free and my body enslaved than my mind enslaved while my body is free." I truly challenge you to dig into that statement and realize how many people we come in contact with on a regular basis who are slaves in their minds yet free in their bodies. This is one of the great travesties of our generation of people. People are unaware of the freedoms that they possess because they have enslaved themselves in their minds. This is what I heard you guard against; one of the main ways that you can battle against this it's through educating yourself and gaining knowledge, and also establishing a vision for your life that is uniquely your own.

Unfortunately, this is one of the hardest things to do because we are so constantly bombarded with messages about keeping up with the Joneses and with so many other superficial things that many of us have not actually taken the time to sit and decide within ourselves what we deem success to actually look like. That you may ask how do I gain this knowledge, how do I educate myself, how do I obtain my vision, and the honest answer is really very simple, the five people that you spend the most time with you will become. So if you want to become something more than the people around you, you have to hang out with people that aren't where you are at, but rather they are where you want to be.

Find Someone to Advise You
One of the best ways to do that is to find someone to mentor you. Oh, and if you aren't into mentorship, then you need to find advisors to have knowledge or strengths in the areas of your weakness. The hard part about that is that often times we are very unaware of our own weaknesses in our own shortcomings, which is why we need a third party to point them out and sometimes help us find a way around them because we have been repeating these things for most of our lives.

You need to surround yourself with people that are going to tell you the truth; some of us struggle with knowing who those people are, and others have gained that knowledge and experience the hard way. If you find that you can't trust yourself and your own opinion of other people to know whether they are trustworthy advisors or people that you want to surround yourself with then, you need to find omeone whom you do trust has that insight for discernment and have them help you pick people that align with where you want to go and what you want to do in life.

My parents were not able to find someone to advise them in the ways that they needed, especially when they needed it most. Do not fall victim to those same circumstances. Go find your tribe. Find the people that you want to surround yourself with that you can grow with, and the people that can advise you honestly; people who have the expertise that you do not. Everyone knows that when you get into business, it's crucial to find a good lawyer, a good banker, and a great accountant.

This is your dream team; when you start out in business, you need to have these people around you to advise you so that you can reach the levels that you want to reach. Ask around, get referrals, and find people in your network to know someone that you can trust. As a Grant Cardone licensee and 10X coach speaker in Mentor, I work with businesses every single day in this capacity helping them grow their businesses, fill in the places and skill sets that they need to be successful in business. Then as a Tax Advisor and strategist I make sure they keep as much of their money in their hands as possible.

The value of mentorship has impacted me personally and enabled me to take my business to heights that I had never dreamed of, as well as allowed me to help people grow their businesses and accomplish their dreams and goals in exponential ways. If you think that you don't need mentorship, I strongly suggest that you reconsider and check your mindset around mentorship because every great athlete has a coach; that's how they're able to make it to those levels and play at those levels consistently, what makes you think that the same amount of effort is not required to be a great entrepreneur and achieve your dreams and goals. The reality is that you need a coach just as much as any athlete.

I would even say that mentorship and discipleship are a necessity for every human being to become or reach even half of their potential. We are communal creatures by nature, and part of living in a community means that we need to learn from one another. We need to support one another in our learning and growing mentorship and discipleship, as well as, finding a closed group of trusted advisors is vital to that growth and attaining the life that you want to live.

A True Leader Gathers Experts

It's not just entrepreneurs that need mentorship and community in order to be successful; in fact, if you look throughout history, The testament how successful a leader can become is inherently dependent on how well they choose their advisors. Every good leader surrounds himself with experts to fill in the places where he lacks and to give him counsel in order to make good decisions and accomplish his goals or her goals. The best leaders ultimately remain students, never suffering their egos and putting that ego above their people.

The ego can be a very dangerous thing; it will oftentimes destroy a relationship and destroy your leadership which is the very thing that the ego is most afraid of happening. To be a great leader, you need to be constantly willing to learn and change and improve because if you are not, that is when you are no longer able to hear wise words from your advisers and experts. That is when you become disconnected from the very people you are there to serve. When this happens, you have two options you can recognize it and start becoming a student again, or you will be forced to recognize it through pain and loss and frustration, and you will inevitably end up losing it all and becoming a student yet again.

The wisest people in the world surround themselves with good counsel. Kings and queens for thousands of years. had royal advisors. Presidents since the founding of America have had advisors and cabinet members help them make the tough calls and decisions that are required of them as part of the job. Business owners have a board of directors that they are responsible to and that help them with the complex decisions that need to be made in business. Pastors will have associate pastors and even mentors themselves to hold them accountable and make sure that they are being faithful to themselves and to God and most of all their congregation.

It's when we operate in a vacuum without these experts or advisors around us, and we are called into leadership that we actually do the most damage, not only to other people but also to ourselves. The bottom line is that you will never be able to accomplish everything you want on your own Grant Cardone says it best; "who's got my money?" It may be a very crass way of saying it at times, but it's true strangers have everything you want in life with that fact being true and relying on what Zig Ziglar is famous for quoting, that "if you help enough people get what they want, you will get what you want". Both of these facts being true. We cannot succeed on our own. We need other people.

And just as we need other people to meet us specifically in business. Oh, they may ask what all this has to do with the tax code or the IRS's Dirty Little Secret, but the truth is we are the secret...each of us is trying to accomplish our dreams in the pursuit of happiness, and each of us can have a part to play in other people's, as well as, our own happiness and the pursuit thereof. At the end of the day, you need to decide whether you are going to be wise, whether you are going to be smart, and whether you are going to seek out the counsel and mentorship of others or are you going to try and do it all on your own? I heard you seek wise counsel.

At the end of the day, remember a rising tide raises all ships. To be the tide that lifts other people up in your life, in your community, ultimately so that their success becomes your success. Learn to leverage the tax code to your benefit, and learn not to fear the IRS but rather use it as a tool that can help you accomplish your goals and dreams. Learn to be an example of the type of community that you would want to be a part of. When your mindset shifts and you begin to look at the tax code differently, at business differently, and at life differently, you will soon realize that someone else's success is also your success.

We do not live in a world of scarcity; we live in a world of abundant and Limitless possibilities. Unfortunately, we limit that abundance and those possibilities because of what's in our minds. I would encourage you to seek out success at yours or Someone else's. You must, above all else, learn, act, and execute. Those three simple things will make all the difference between where your life is and where you end up; this mindset will save you in hard times, it will sustain you, and keep you humble in Good Times.

It will make sure that when others are sinking around you that your ship and those in your circle will stay afloat and can even put you in the position where when your mindset is correct, and your skill set can back it up, you will be able to save people from drowning. There is no better feeling. Let me assure you, then brings someone back from the brink of failure and show them a path to success. The hardest part is that not everyone will take it. The question is, will you?

> *"Success is the difference between where you are and where you could be."*
> *-Grant Cardone*

Thank You

First of all, I want to thank you for picking up this book. I hope that you find something within its pages that changes your journey and your trajectory in life. If nothing else, I hope you find it a good read; if it doesn't change your life, that's fine. The things I've recounted in the things that I speak about are things that are and have changed the course of my life forever. No two people are the same, and no two people have the same destiny, but if there is a part of my experience and my knowledge that can help just one other person live out their dream, I am satisfied with every hardship I've had to endure.

Through every heartbreak, through every failed business, through hospitalizations through marriage and divorce, through bankruptcy and foreclosure through birth and through death. There has been no shortage of obstacles overcome in my life, but I will use the overcoming of all of these obstacles to help people. So I hope this book has helped you in some small way, even if that way is just to bring a smile or laugh. I truly thank you for your time from the bottom of my heart, and I look forward to any chance encounter we may have met there, here, there, or in the air.

Sincerely,

Patrick A. Rood
The Tax Wizard

The Cover Photo has a story. It is from the U.S. National Archives. It is Original Artwork for World War II Posters
Created by: NARA & DVIDS Public Domain Archive
Dated: 1941
Uncle Sam (Information on the back: Pd for. Not used. Rejected.) [Robert S. Sloan]
Original Artwork for World War II Posters

Link for credit above
https://nara.getarchive.net/media/uncle-sam-information-on-the-back-pd-for-not-used-rejected-robert-s-sloan-cdb23f

I don't have the time to write up the story, but it is interesting and was to be added here.

1st article to take from
https://text-message.blogs.archives.gov/2019/09/19/the-uncle-sam-poster-for-the-security-of-war-information-campaign-and-the-one-that-never-was/

2nd article to take from
https://blog.nuclearsecrecy.com/2012/03/23/friday-image-uncle-sam-says-shush/

THE IRS – Dirty Little Secrets

www.ingramcontent.com/pod-product-compliance
Lightning Source LLC
Chambersburg PA
CBHW020753230426
43665CB00009B/577